JAZZ KEYBOARD TOOLBOX

BILL CUNLIFFE

The Nuts and Bolts Guide to Learning Jazz Keyboard

I'd like to thank Jeff Clayton, Tom Warrington and
Mark Ferber for their sensitive, swinging playing;
Talley Sherwood for his great engineering,
Richard Barron at Sonora Studios; and especially
Link Harnsberger, Sharon Aaronson, Kate Westin,
Bruce Goldes and Kim Kasabian at Alfred for their
incredible hard work and support.

Cover illustration: *Great Balls o' Fire*
1992, Mixed Media Gil Mayers, Super Stock

CONTENTS

INTRODUCTION

Although there are many books about jazz theory for the pianist, you don't need that much theory to go out there and play and have a good time. A solid knowledge of just a few basic tools and the intuitive experience of playing with a rhythm section is much better than a whole lot of book study and no playing experience. Therefore, this book is intended to introduce some of the most important concepts in keyboard playing to the aspiring jazz pianist:

- *comping*, which is providing a strong, harmonically accurate and rhythmically swinging accompaniment in a group jazz setting, and

- *soloing*, which is playing improvised lines with the right hand as solos.

To do this, you need to learn the basics of jazz harmony—just enough to allow you to play simple 12-bar blues tunes for now. With this knowledge, you can practice with the rhythm section on the enclosed CD, and later start to play simple pop and jazz standards. The *voicings* (arrangement of notes in a chord) and soloing

Thelonious Monk
From the 1940s to the 1970s, Thelonious Monk was one of the true innovators of jazz piano. He composed several great 12-bar blues tunes including "Blue Monk," and "Straight No Chaser."

concepts learned in this book will apply in some way to every form of improvised jazz and pop music.

This method stresses the ear; you'll be given just enough theory to understand what you are doing so that you can do it yourself. But the entire book can be studied even if you don't have any previous knowledge of theory—you can just read the musical examples and play them along with the CD until they are memorized. Furthermore, if your music-reading skills aren't that great, you can just listen to the CD and imitate the melodies and voicings that you hear. If you do this, you will have most of the skills you need to play simple song forms in jazz.

If you are new to jazz, you might want to go through the book several times in this suggested order:

- First, learn the melodies and voicings in the book and on the CD. This will give you enough musical artillery to create great sounding voicings, comp with a rhythm section, and to begin to solo on jazz tunes.

- Then, go back to the beginning and work on the special IMPROVISING TIPS given in each chapter. These tips offer advanced information that will help you get a more authentic jazz sound in your soloing.

- Finally, put the book aside and just jam with the CD. If you are having fun, you are learning what you need to learn!

Historical Perspective

In the early days of jazz, the pianist was an orchestra unto him(her)self. The melody, harmony and rhythm of the tune were all contained in the two busy hands of the performer. In the 1920s and 1930s, players like James P. Johnson, Fats Waller and the boogie-woogie pianists like Albert Ammons and Meade Lux Lewis amazed crowds with their abilities to keep an awesome groove, invent swinging melodies and drive a band all by themselves. This type of playing was often called *stride* piano, as the left hand strode between bass notes and chords.

The great Art Tatum (1910–1956) made solo jazz piano playing a musical and technical feat equal to that of the great 19th-century improvisers of classical music, like Sergei Rachmaninoff and Franz Liszt. But by the time the 1940s rolled around, the quick tempos and changing roles of the bass player and drummer in a jazz group required the pianist to play in a different way. Through pianists such as Bud Powell (1924–1966) and later, Red Garland (1923–1984) and Bill Evans (1929–1980), a different approach evolved, which is the foundation of all contemporary jazz piano styles.

- Pianists left the bass notes out, to be played by the bassist in a style that became known as the *walking bass* (quarter notes that outlined the harmonies of the tune).

- The chords were simplified to voicings of three or four notes, which were rhythmically comped. Pianists selected only the notes in the chord that would show the harmonic movement as simply as possible, freeing themselves to focus on their more intricate bebop lines in the right hand.

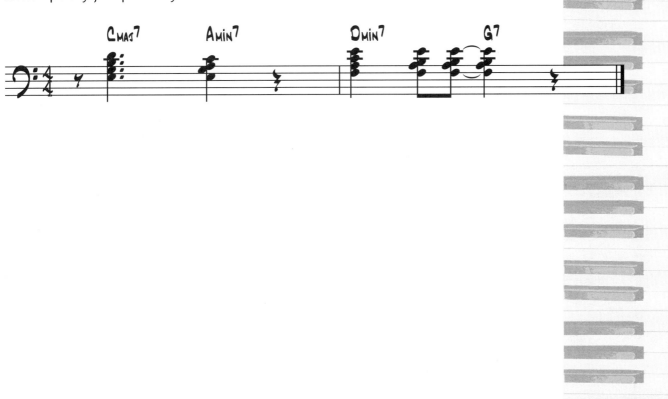

Chord Symbols

In pop and jazz music, chord symbols are used as a shorthand way of indicating the possible voicings that can be played by the left hand (or both hands, if a pianist is in a band accompanying another instrument). To read chord symbols, it is helpful to know a little about basic musical intervals, triads (three-note chords) and 7th chords, and how they relate to the major scale. If you prefer to read music that is written out for both hands, simply skip ahead and read the examples in each section as you play along with the CD.

The diagrams below show intervals, triads and 7th chords in the key of C major. These will help you identify the material you'll cover from this point on:

Major and Minor Intervals

PERFECT UNISON   MINOR 2ND   MAJOR 2ND   MINOR 3RD

MAJOR 3RD   PERFECT 4TH   AUGMENTED 4TH OR DIMINISHED 5TH

PERFECT 5TH   AUGMENTED 5TH OR MINOR 6TH   MAJOR 6TH

MINOR 7TH   MAJOR 7TH   PERFECT OCTAVE

Triads in C Major

C	Dmin	Emin	F	G	Amin	Bdim	C
I	ii	iii	IV	V	vi	vii	I
TONIC	SUBDOMINANT FUNCTION		SUBDOMINANT	DOMINANT			

Seventh Chords in C Major

Cmaj7	Dmin7	Emin7	Fmaj7	G7	Amin7	Bmin7(b5)	Cmaj7
I	ii	iii	IV	V	vi	vii	I
TONIC	SUBDOMINANT FUNCTION		SUBDOMINANT	DOMINANT			

The following three chords will be used in the text:

- ## The major 7th chord

  The C major 7th chord is spelled C, E, G and B. It is made up of a major triad (C, E and G) with a major 7th (B) added above the root. This chord symbol is written as Cmaj7, CM7 or C$^\triangle$7.

- ## The minor 7th chord

  The C minor 7th chord is spelled C, E♭, G and B♭. The E♭ is a minor 3rd above the root. The B♭ is a minor 7th above the root. This chord symbol is written as Cmin7, Cm7, or C–7.

- ## The dominant 7th chord

  The C dominant 7th chord is spelled C, E, G and B♭. The E is a major 3rd above the root, and the B♭ is a minor 7th above. It is called the dominant 7th because it dominates, or requires resolution to, a major triad or major 7th chord; for example, G7 (G, B, D, F) wants to resolve to Cmaj7 (C, E, G, B). Try this on the piano. The dominant 7th chord symbol is written simply as C7.

The minor 7th chord often functions as a subdominant or lead-in to the dominant 7th chord. So, in jazz, we often see Dmin7 (D, F, A, C) to G7 (G, B, D, F) to Cmaj7 (C, E, G, B). This is called the **ii-V-I** progression, and it is ever-present in jazz music. Roman numerals are capitalized to show that the chords are major or dominant, and lowercase letters are used to show chords that are minor. By the way, for you Curious Georges, classical harmony from Bach to Brahms works exactly the same way, only the **IV** chord (in the key of C, this is Fmaj7: F, A, C, E) is often used in classical music instead of the **ii** chord (Dmin7), which is more often used in jazz. In classical music, both the **ii-V-I** and **IV-V-I** function as subdominant to dominant to tonic. Same stuff, different terminology. (You don't really need to know this, but I thought it was interesting.)

The rule for developing hip modern jazz piano voicings is that you start with the 3rd and 7th only and build up the voicing from there. So the Cmaj7 chord would be voiced in the left hand with E and B; either note could be above the other.

The Cmin7 chord would be voiced with E♭ and B♭.

The C7 chord would be voiced with E and B♭.

In terms of making the voicing sound authentic, the left hand ranges between the C below middle C and the C above middle C.

This is the clearest register for harmony; any lower and the voicing sounds muddy, any higher and the harmony interferes with the right-hand leads. You will get all this information intuitively if you play along with and eventually memorize the voicings in the book.

How to Play with the Tracks

Each lesson starts with a tune, which is played by the rhythm section on the CD a number of times. The CD has drums and bass on both channels. Piano is on the left channel and saxophone is on the right.

- Following a count-off, simply read the notes on the staff. Starting with the two-note 3rd and 7th voicings, you can play along with the piano part until you are comfortable with the voicings, then simply turn off the left channel and play your new voicings along with the bass and drums.

- Once you have learned how to do this, start playing the melody along with the pianist on the CD. You can read the melody from the book, or you can just listen and "cop" the melody that is played. It's often best to do this by ear because you are listening not only to the melody, but also to the phrasing and articulation, and to the overall vibe of the rhythm section.

It's absolutely fine to find the best way that works for you. As you go along, you will be presented with different suggestions.

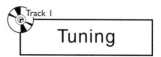

Track 1

Tuning

Comping

The word *comping* is believed to have come from the word "accompanying," but it could also have come from the word "complementing," as in complementing what the soloist does. This means to provide a supportive and interesting background texture for the solo line. In addition to the harmonic role of outlining the changes, there are four basic rhythmic roles for the comper, which, in this case, is your left hand.

- You can play whole and half notes (or "footballs," as they are called in the studios). I suggest that you learn how to comp this way first.

- Second, you can comp in the holes left by the right-hand melody or solo, so that at any moment only one hand is playing. In this way, the two hands trade off or engage in dialogue with each other.

- Third, the left hand can mimic the right hand rhythmically. Here both hands play the same rhythms at the same time. The left hand is free to simplify if the right-hand lead is very active.

- Finally, in what is called *vamping*, the left hand can play a repeated figure. This is especially common in pop and Latin music.

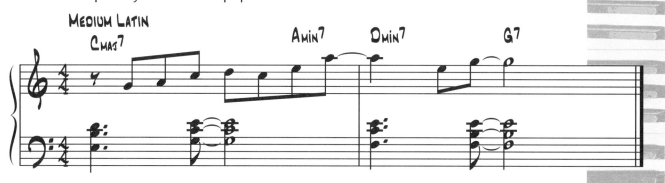

Further examples will follow in the text.

A Word about Right-Hand Lines

You will study left-hand comping for the first few lessons, then right-hand lead playing will be introduced. As you learn this, it is often helpful to practice the right-hand leads separately with the rhythm section until you are comfortable and really enjoying yourself. Then add the left hand, incorporating what you have learned in your comping.

In developing right-hand lines, you will start out with the basics of the blues scale and then move into chord/scale concepts. It is very important for you to start listening to great jazz players and try to incorporate aspects of what they do into your own improvisations. A discography appears at the back of the book.

Photo: Institute of Jazz Studies

Bud Powell
During the 1940s, Bud Powell was the first pianist to cop the melodic styles of Charlie Parker and Dizzy Gillespie. He also created an exciting style of his own.

SECTION 1

Two-Note Left-Hand Jazz Voicings

TOOL 1 : Standard Blues

What is normally called the blues in jazz today is a 12-bar progression that is also frequently found in pop music. It is in ¾ time and is based on a poetic scheme derived from the founders of jazz and blues at the beginning of the 20th century:

Goin' to Yuba City, Yuba City here I come.
Goin' to Yuba City, Yuba City here I come.
They got great little tacos there, and I'm a gonna get me one.

© 1999 Bill Cunliffe Music

As you can see, the blues is a chord progression and melody, which is played in three four-bar phrases. This is the typical sequence of chords used to accompany the melody, simplified here for our needs.

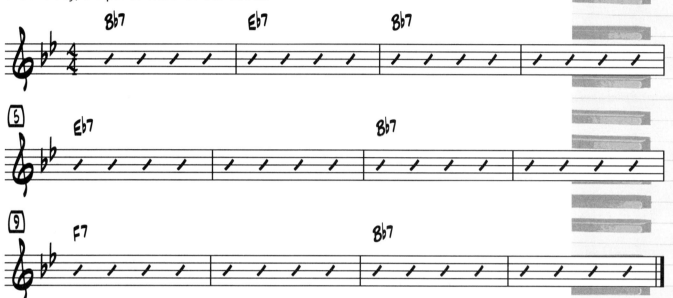

Basically Blues is a 12-bar blues in a medium swing groove. The first voicing you are going to learn is the two-note 3rd and 7th voicing. Sometimes the 3rd is on top, sometimes the 7th is on top; they alternate to keep the voicings close to each other and sounding smooth as the chords change. If you read the left-hand voicings, you can play them throughout the track and you'll sound just fine—or you can even listen without reading; try to hear what notes the pianist is playing in the left hand, and match them at the piano. If you are adventurous, you can learn the right-hand melody by playing along with the pianist on the CD (it's best to start with just one hand at a time, so leave out the

left hand as you do this), and eventually put the left hand in there.

Each track in **Tools 1–6** will play the basic melody twice, then leave it out for three choruses, just comping, and then play the melody once more so you can practice. Remember, if you are having trouble, just go back to the basic left hand.

Notice that Jeff "interprets" the melody on the saxophone, adding bends and slurs before and after certain notes. It's always good for a pianist to imitate the sound of a horn—this makes your melodies "sing." I often literally sing with my playing, and breathe during the rests.

IMPROVISING TIP:

The B♭ blues scale can be used for creating right-hand lines. You can play these six notes through all the chord changes of the blues and you'll never be wrong! Practice this with different rhythms using quarter notes, 8th notes, triplet 8ths, or any rhythms you hear.

B♭ BLUES SCALE

TOOL 2 : ii-V-I Blues

PLAY 6 TIMES

play "off" melody (see next page) — fit together — coherent

BEBOP BLUES Track 3

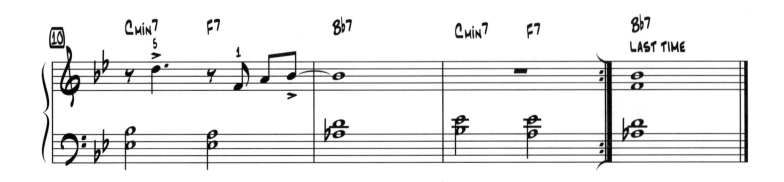

Bebop Blues is also a 12-bar blues in a medium swing groove. You are going to use the same two-note 3rd and 7th voicing you used in **Tool 1**, but you are now going to add a few substitute changes. The most common substitution is the addition of a **ii7** chord in front of a **V7** chord.

For example, in bar 10, instead of a whole bar of F7 (the **V7** chord in the key of B♭ major), Charlie Parker would have substituted two beats of Cmin7 (the **ii7** chord) and two beats of F7 (the **V7** chord), as was done here. This is called a **ii-V**.

If the progression were to move to B♭maj7 (the **I** chord), it would be called a **ii-V-I**. This can be done on any **V7** chord, so instead of a whole bar of B♭7 (bar 4), you can substitute two beats of Fmin7 in front of the two beats of B♭7. Any chord that is a dominant chord (e.g., B♭7, E♭7, F7) can be substituted in this way.

The **ii7** chord voicing is constructed in the same way as the **V7** voicing, using the 3rd and 7th, except that in the **ii7** chord, the 3rd is minor (flatted). On a Cmin7 chord, the notes used are E♭ and B♭. Sometimes the 3rd will be on top, sometimes the 7th. Don't worry about this. Just play what is written and feel free to reverse the order of the notes if you like. If they are basically in the middle of the keyboard (around middle C) they will sound fine. If you want to add notes to the left-hand voicing, such as the 5th or 6th, or just explore, go ahead. As long as the basic 3rd and 7th are there, whatever you play will sound pretty good. Practice this piece the same way you did the first time—start with either hand alone if you like, and then put them together. It's important here to make sure your 8th notes are *swinging*. To play swing 8ths, practice each group of two 8ths as a triplet figure:

Then you accent the "and" of each beat like this:

And spend some time listening and emulating the phrasing of the melody on the CD.

Improvising Tip:

When you are improvising on the blues scale, try throwing in parts of the melody from time to time. For example, play the blues scale in bars 1–4, the melody in bars 5–8 and the blues scale the rest of the way. Or alternate two bars of blues scale, two bars of melody. The possibilities are really endless, and you'll be learning new stuff for improvising.

TOOL 3 : Minor Blues

TRANE'S BLUES  Track 4

Play 6 times

Medium swing

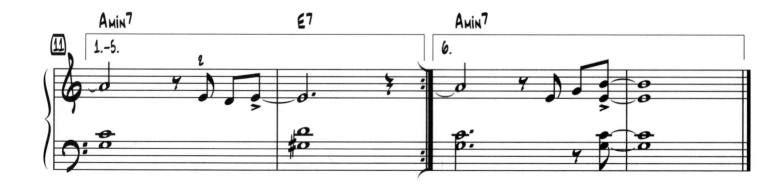

Trane's Blues is a 12-bar blues form in a minor key. Although this is not a new form in jazz, it was John Coltrane who really popularized it among players with his tune "Mr. P.C." from his album *Giant Steps* (Atlantic).

Practice this tune hands separately like the others, starting this one with the left hand, then changing to the right-hand melody, and then putting hands together.

IMPROVISING TIP:

Although this is in a minor key (A minor), you can still improvise on the A blues scale in the right hand at any time, and you'll always sound fine. You can also alternate bars of blues scale with bars of melody, just as you did in **Tool 2**.

Another way of improvising is to take the melody and vary it. Here are two basic ways to do this:

- Change the rhythm of the melody.

- Add ornaments to the melody. (An ornament is a new note added to a melody note from immediately above or below it.)

A Blues Scale

Here is an example of a chorus of blues playing "off" the melody that does these two things. There's no need to worry or think about harmony here; just move notes around rhythmically. As long as you keep close to the written melody, you are always OK.

SECTION 2

Three-Note Left-Hand Jazz Voicings

TOOL 4 : Standard Blues

BASICALLY BLUES 2 Track 5

PLAY 6 TIMES

Basically Blues 2 is a similar progression to the track used in **Tool 1**, with an additional note added to the two-note voicing. The new note, besides the 3rd and 7th, is either the 5th or 9th, depending on the register.

The 9th is a new color tone that, in the **V7** chord, can be natural (an octave and a whole step above the bass), flatted (lowered a half step from the ♮9th) or sharped (raised a half step from the ♮9th). In the major and minor chords the 9th is always natural.

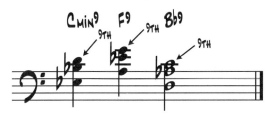

In the **V7** chords in this tune, the 9ths that are used in the voicings are always ♭9ths, to help you get used to the new sound. Often the chord symbol is written as B♭7 rather than B♭9, but you're free to add 9ths in your voicings even if they're not part of the chord symbol.

If the 3rd is above the 7th, the 5th would normally be added above the 3rd to create a spread in the left-hand voicing (a wider voiced chord).

If the 7th is above the 3rd, the 9th is added above the 7th (see bar 2)—again, to make the chord a little wider. But in the B♭7 chords, notice that the 6th is substituted for the 5th in the voicing (see bar 1) throughout the tune. This creates a real cool rub in the chord between the 6th and the 7th in the lower octave.

In addition, some *anticipations* have been added in the left hand. This means that a downbeat chord is moved to the previous 8th note, usually on the "and" of 4 (see bars 3, 6, 8 and 10). When a chord changes on beat 3, you often play the new chord on the "and" of beat 2. Often, accented or offbeat notes in the melody are supported with left-hand chords (see the end of bars 10 and 13)—not all the time, just occasionally to create some interest.

Practice the hands separately, and then put them together.

IMPROVISING TIP:

Continue to use the blues scale for your right-hand improvising. Get to know this new melody well enough so you can alternate between playing parts of the melody and improvising the blues scale WITHOUT LOOKING AT THE MUSIC. Also, go back and play along with **Tools 1–3** until you can do it without looking at the paper. If you always read the music, you will never truly know it. Great jazz players always memorize as much as they can. That way they can look at the cute girls (or guys!) in the audience.

TOOL 5 : ii-V-I Blues

Bebop Blues 2   Track 6

PLAY 6 TIMES

MEDIUM SWING

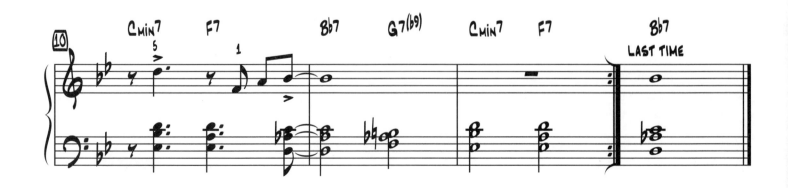

You will now become familiar with one of the most important alterations in bebop—the ♭5 (flatted 5th). This is often used in the ii7 chord, and it becomes the ♭9 in the related **V7** chord (in a G7 chord, A♭ is the ♭9).

This tune is built on a blues progression similar to the tune you encountered in **Tool 2**, but with three-note voicings (like **Tool 4**). Notice that in the beginning of bar 8, the register of the melody is so low that a standard 3-7-9 voicing would get in its way.

Use a 3-5-7 voicing instead, which reinforces the ♭5 in the melody on the **ii** chord. Keep in mind that the 5th could have been left out, because with the always-important 3rd and 7th in the voicing, the chord sounds strong without the 5th.

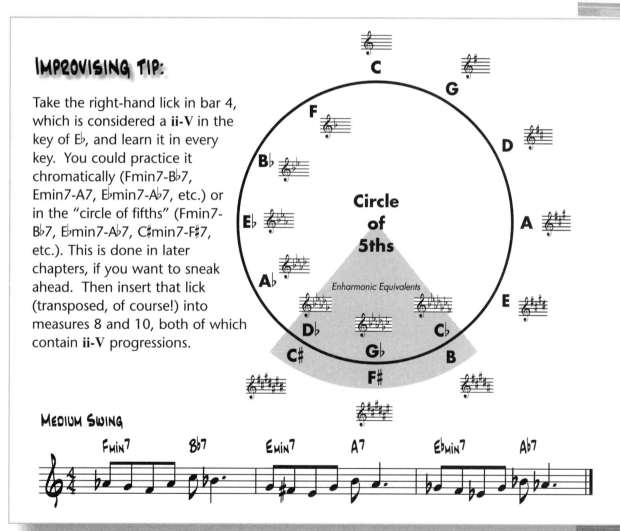

IMPROVISING TIP:

Take the right-hand lick in bar 4, which is considered a **ii-V** in the key of E♭, and learn it in every key. You could practice it chromatically (Fmin7-B♭7, Emin7-A7, E♭min7-A♭7, etc.) or in the "circle of fifths" (Fmin7-B♭7, E♭min7-A♭7, C♯min7-F♯7, etc.). This is done in later chapters, if you want to sneak ahead. Then insert that lick (transposed, of course!) into measures 8 and 10, both of which contain **ii-V** progressions.

For further study:

Learn a couple of other blues tunes, for example:

- "Billie's Bounce" by Charlie Parker (*Complete Savoy Sessions*, Savoy)
- "Tenor Madness" by Sonny Rollins (*Tenor Madness*, Original Jazz Classics)

- "Walkin'" as recorded by Miles Davis (*Walkin'*, Original Jazz Classics)

Check out the versions from the mid-1950s, as they're not played at such a breakneck tempo as the later recordings.

TOOL 6 : Minor Blues

PLAY 6 TIMES

TRANE'S BLUES 2  Track 7

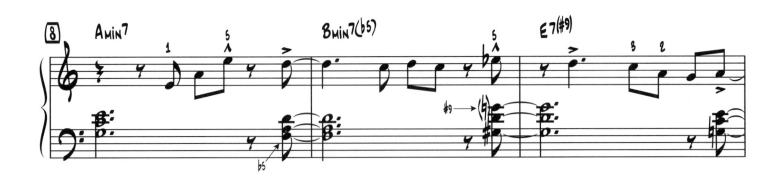

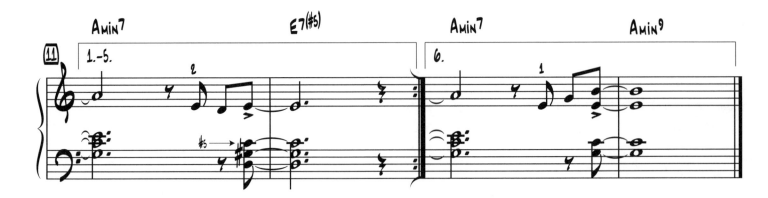

This is a similar progression to the track used in **Tool 3**, but now you are adding either a 5th or 9th to the two-note voicing. Notice in the chord that leads into bar 10 (E7(♯9)) that it looks like a minor 3rd has been added on top of the E7 voicing with the major 3rd and minor 7th. This is called the ♯9 (sharp nine, sometimes written as +9), and it's a characteristic sound of jazz. Don't worry about enharmonic spellings in jazz—we street guys use them all the time. Regardless of whether the note is spelled F𝄪 or G, it still sounds the same. The **V7** chords are the only type of chords in which a ♯9 and ♭9 can be used. The cool thing is that on a **V7**, you can use EITHER ♯9 or ♭9, or BOTH ♯9 and ♭9, and it sounds really great. (But don't use the ♮9 in conjunction with either the ♯9 or ♭9!)

In **Tool 5** you flatted the 5th and in this section you sharped the 5th (C♮ is the ♯5 in the E7 chord that leads into bar 12). The rules for sharping or flatting the 5ths are similar to the rules for the 9ths: on a dominant (**V7**) chord you can use ♭5 and ♯5 together, but you can't use a ♮5 with either of them.

And the ♭5 is common in tonic (**Imaj7**, often referred to as the ♯11) and subdominant (**ii7**) chords as well.

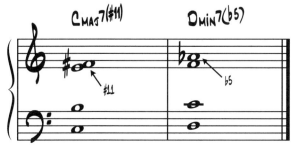

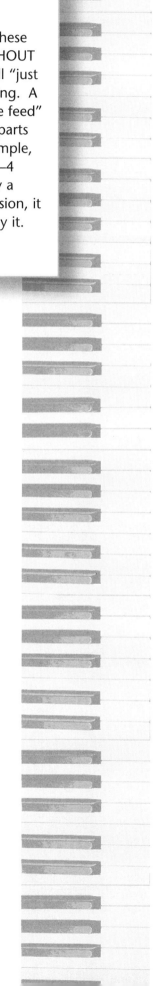

IMPROVISING TIP:

It's really important to memorize these tunes. Once you know them WITHOUT LOOKING AT THE CHART, they will "just occur" to you as you are improvising. A good intermediate step is to "force feed" parts of the melody into different parts of the chord progression. For example, you can play the melody of bars 1–4 over bars 5–8. Since it's essentially a blues melody over a blues progression, it will work no matter where you play it.

For further study:
Find another minor blues tune and learn the melody by heart. You can even try to play it over the track. "Mr. P.C." by John Coltrane is a good suggestion (you would have to transpose it to A minor, as the original is in C minor). Here are a few other suggestions:

- "Equinox" by John Coltrane (*Coltrane's Sound*, Atlantic)

- "Nutville" by Horace Silver (*Cape Verdean Blues*, Blue Note)

TOOL 7 : Chord Substitutions

PLAY 6 TIMES

PARKER'S BLUES Track 8

This track is a 12-bar blues using more sophisticated chord substitutions, like those employed by saxophonist Charlie Parker in his tunes "Blues for Alice" (*Confirmation: Best of the Verve Years*) and "Sippin' at Bells." (*Bird/The Savoy Recordings/Master Takes*).

Now here's a new form of harmonic substitution that was pioneered by the great pianist Art Tatum and further developed by Charlie Parker and pianists Bud

Powell and Thelonious Monk. In bars 7 and 8, the original progression (a bar of Amin7 followed by a bar of D7) is replaced by two beats of Amin7 and two beats of D7 in bar 7, and two beats of A♭min7 and two beats of D♭7 in bar 8. Although the resolution of the D♭7 to Gmin7 is unusual, the progression works because of the overall motion of the bass line: Amin7 to A♭min7 to Gmin7 (the downbeats of bars 7, 8 and 9).

Another thing that is going on here is the use of chord substitution in the *turnaround*. This is the part of the tune in the last two measures, where the progression starts on the **I7** chord (F7 in bar 11) and goes to the **V7** in the last bar (C7 in bar 12), which resolves to the **I7** at the top of the next chorus (F7). In bars 11 and 12, instead of F7 | C7, you can substitute F7 | Gmin7, C7, and then add a chord a 5th away from the Gmin7 like this: F7, D7 | Gmin7, C7.

F7	C7		F7
F7	Gmin7	C7	F7
F7 D7	Gmin7	C7	F7

Practice this progression until the left hand is pretty much going on auto-pilot. Then practice the right hand by itself. Then put them together.

Notice in bar 8, the melody note G is the ♭5 chord tone of the D♭7 chord. The ♭5 melody and chord tones are often considered ♯11s, especially when they occur in the melody one and one-half octaves above the bass in major 7th and dominant 7th chords. When they are found in minor 7th chords, they are always referred to as ♭5s, regardless of the octave in which they occur. The ♯11 and ♭5 designations are often included as part of the chord symbols, for example, D♭7(♯11), Cmaj7(♯11) and Dmin7(♭5). Often Dmin7(♭5) is referred to as D∅7. Sorry, I told you some of this didn't make sense!!!

IMPROVISING TIP: Play along with the melody until you can play it easily, then practice the following exercise:

- Using the rhythm of the melody, play the roots of each chord in the right hand. Not only will this help you hear the roots when you are not playing them in the left hand, but it will help you start to think of your voicings as being two handed, which will help later when you are accompanying horn players and singers.

In this and following lessons, I play a solo after the first comping chorus (here, I play the written example below), giving you one more comping chorus afterwards.

SECTION 3
Chord-Scale Patterns, Right Hand

TOOL 8 : ii-V-I Blues

Bebop Blues 3   Track 9

PLAY 6 TIMES

Now that you are comfortable with the basic left-hand chord voicings, it's time to get into some hipper right-hand leads. As described below, you will start to practice spelling out each change in the blues by outlining chords using right hand patterns.

The pattern that you will use is made up of chord tones 1-3-5-7-5-3-1—up and down each chord. Practicing this pattern will help you to get used to hearing the correct notes played in the right hand that go with your left-hand voicings. Once you can do that, you are really free to create melodies that reflect the chord changes accurately. Notice that when there are two chords per bar, you just run each chord up to the 7th and move on to the next chord.

In this track for the basic blues changes, the rhythm section is playing some hipper stuff to challenge you. Simply play the right-hand example by itself over the track until you can play it WITHOUT LOOKING AT THE MUSIC. Then add the written-out left hand. If you practiced the previous lessons thoroughly, you won't need to look at the music. If you do need to look at the music, GO BACK and review the voicings in **Tool 4** until they're memorized. Then it will be easy to add

the right hand. When you are not looking at the music anymore, you are a master!

Once you have learned this, play along with the track; and listen to the track, NOT TO YOURSELF! If you are listening to the track as you are playing and things seem to be going along well, THEY ARE! Dig it.

In my solo, I use the blues scale exclusively. Notice the use of triplets as well as swing 8th notes.

In playing leads, accent the "ands" of each beat as I have notated for you. And there is usually a hard staccato accent at the end of each line. Keep feeling "triplet 8ths," but be aware that at faster tempos, the 8ths become more even. Just listen to the ride cymbal of the drummer and imitate that feel. Following these hints will make your lines more "jazzy."

Notice that the **V7** chords that substitute the 6th for the 5th are called "13th" chords (see bars 2, 10 and 12). A 13th chord doesn't require the 9th or 11th, but the 7th always needs to be there. For example, F13 = F, A, C, E♭ with the D (the 13th) a 7th above the E♭, leaving out the 5th (C) and root (F).

IMPROVISING TIP:

If playing 1–3–5–7–5–3–1 is easy for you, try doing the same exercise starting from the 7th down. Start by just playing the 7th in the right hand and the chord voicing in the left. When you can play that easily, run the chord 7-5-3-1-3-5-7.

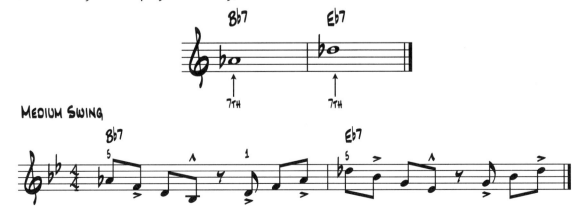

TOOL 9 : Minor Blues

TRANE'S BLUES 3   🎵 Track 10

PLAY 6 TIMES

MEDIUM SWING

Here's the same pattern as **Tool 8**, except in a minor blues. Start on the root, going up and back down (1-3-5-7-5-3-1). When that is mastered, practice playing the 7th in the right hand in half and whole notes along with each change in the left hand. When you can do that, try playing 7-5-3-1-3-5-7 on each change (if there were two changes per bar, the pattern would be 7-5-3-1, 7-5-3-1).

Remember: get away from looking at the page as quickly as you can. And remember to accent the "ands" of each beat and listen to the ride cymbal … make your 8th notes blend into the drummer's.

In soloing on the minor blues, the regular blues scale works just fine. In my solo I tried to do some "sliding" into notes from below—this is an important part of the blues sound.

IMPROVISING TIP:

Now, let's go for some hip stuff. Play the 9th of each chord in the right hand along with the written chord voicing in the left.

If you find this difficult, just practice the right hand alone. When you are fluent at this, start on the 9th and work your way down to the 3rd (9-7-5-3-5-7-9). Then reverse it (3-5-7-9-7-5-3). Practice whichever sequence is easiest for you first, then learn the other.

MEDIUM SWING

You are closer then ever to the bebop gods' ultimate dream: 8th notes at any tempo!

TOOL 10 : 3rds and 7ths — The Hippest Notes

PARKER'S BLUES 2   Track 11

PLAY 6 TIMES

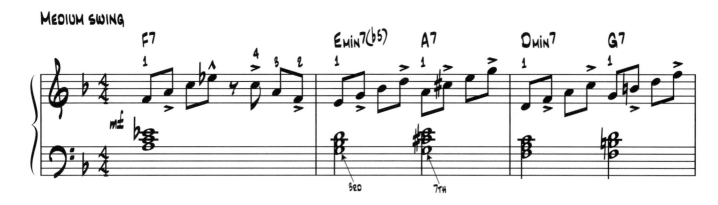

Here's the same pattern as in the previous chapters, but now, in addition, let's practice playing the 3rds and 7ths of each change.

Notice that you will be doubling one of the notes of the chord voicing in the left hand. It's essential for any improviser to pick out the 3rd and 7th of each change, and improvise off of those notes.

I tried in my solo to incorporate some 1-3-5-7 stuff over the changes, as the blues scale by itself won't work in a blues with a lot of **ii-V** progressions.

IMPROVISING TIP:

Try playing the rhythm of the melody, by playing the 9th of each chord as you did in **Tool 7** with the roots of the chords. You can stick with ♮9ths all the way through at first. Then try doing it with ♭9ths on the dominant chords. Then do it with ♯9ths. For those of you who are adventurous, find the ♭5th (or ♯11!) of each dominant chord and play the rhythm of the melody with that note. You can use the ♮11th (which is an octave and a 4th above the bass) with the minor 7th chords. This sounds really hip, and paves the way for some very interesting melodic gestures later on.

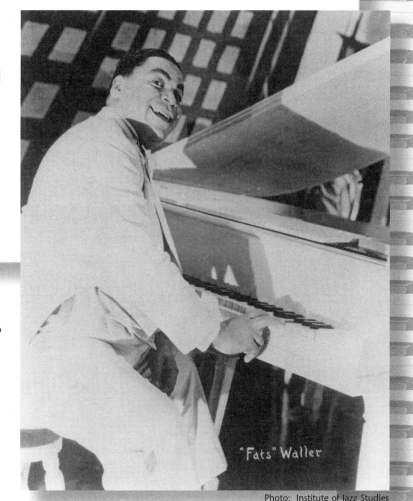

Fats Waller
Fats Waller (1904–1943) is arguably the most swinging solo pianist of all time, and undoubtedly the funniest.

Photo: Institute of Jazz Studies

SECTION 4

Three-Note Voicings, Standard Tune Forms

TOOL 11 : Rock Vamp 1 with Blues Scale

SOMETHING FOR HERBIE *Track 12*

PLAY 5 TIMES

MEDIUM FUNKY JAZZ-ROCK

The transcription of the piano solo played on the recording of *Something for Herbie* can be found on page 44.

* IN JAZZ, THE SMALL NOTES (GRACE NOTES) ARE TO BE PLAYED <u>ON</u> THE BEAT. THEY CAN BE OMITTED AT THE PLAYER'S DISCRETION.

You have done well, if you are here. You now have all the resources to play the heck out of a jazz-rock tune. There are fewer changes in these tunes than in the music you've been playing so far.

So, practice hands separately at first, and then put them together. In this example the melody will be played once, then you do your thing either with the C blues scale, improvising "off the melody," or running the chord changes as you have done in **Tools 8–10**. It all works and it's all good. Then, as soon as you can, put away the music and jam with the track.

This tune is stylistically like Herbie Hancock's "Watermelon Man" (from *Takin' Off*, Blue Note), probably the first

great jazz-rock tune. Remember, if you are not a great reader, take heart! It's often just as good to learn the tune by listening to the CD and copying the tune that way. Some of the really great jazz players were mediocre readers who were forced to develop fantastic ears.

Here I play the C blues scale throughout the tune (even through the F7) using some real typical "blues licks." Try to copy a few of these and learn them in some other keys.

Notice the C7 chord with a G bass in bar 15. Here, you can play C7 in the left hand or, if you are comping with both hands, play a C7 voicing in the right hand and the G bass in the left hand.

IMPROVISING TIP:

You can *blow* (improvise) on the C blues scale throughout the tune or you can try the F blues scale in bars 9–14. Notice that the melody of the tune uses both scales.

C BLUES SCALE

F BLUES SCALE

TOOL 12 : Rock Vamp 2 with Dorian Scale

MINOR GROOVE   Track 13

Here's another simple jazz-rock tune, only this one is in the minor mode. Since it has a bluesy melody, but is not the 12-bar blues form, you can use the

C blues scale to improvise on the Cmin7 chord, but you will have to transpose the scale when the chord changes to B♭min7.

- Bars 1–4 (intro), 5–12 (first 8 bars of the tune), and 17–end: improvise on the C blues scale.

- Bars 9–12: improvise on the B♭ blues scale.

C BLUES SCALE

B♭ BLUES SCALE

IMPROVISING TIP:

A scale that works well with a tune like this is the Dorian scale, which is like the natural minor (the minor that comes from the key signature), but with a raised 6th (see below). You can also think of the Dorian as starting on the second degree of a major scale.

For example, C Dorian is the B♭ major scale, starting on C. Again, you would play 8 bars of C Dorian followed by 4 bars of B♭ Dorian, and 4 bars of C Dorian.

I use the C Dorian scale a lot in my solo, and throw a blues lick in from time to time.

C DORIAN SCALE

B♭ DORIAN SCALE

Herbie Hancock
An important jazz pianist and composer, Herbie Hancock created lush, complex voicings and comped in a very hip, rhythmically fresh style. From the late 1960s, he was musically innovative through his use of several synthesizers such as the Moog, the Arp, the Clavinet and the Vocoder (pictured).

Photo: Institute of Jazz Studies

TOOL 13 : Latin Two-Chord Vamp with Blues Scale

Since Latin jazz is so popular today, here's something in that vein with a left-hand vamp figure. Two-chord vamps are characteristic in this style. Notice that the first eight bars of the melody (bars 5–12) and the last four (bars 17–end) are based entirely on the G blues scale.

G BLUES SCALE

Bars 13–16 are a **ii-V** of the Gmin7 chord in bar 17. So you can play the entire tune using the G blues scale.

Remember that the 8th notes are usually *straight* ("straight 8ths" means to play them evenly) in Latin jazz, but they can be a bit "triplety," especially in more jazzy bossa nova style tunes (think Blue Note early 60s stuff, like Kenny Dorham's *Una Mas* and Lee Morgan's *Sidewinder*). Accents and articulation are very important, just as much as in swing/bebop jazz.

Ay arriba!!

IMPROVISING TIP:

Because the entire tune circles around the key of G minor, the G Dorian scale works throughout. You can also practice the chord patterns from previous lessons on each change (1-3-5-7-5-3-1, 7-5-3-1-3-5-7, 3-5-7-9-7-5-3, and 9-7-5-3-5-7-9).

Even though this is a more Latin-tinged tune, I use the blues scale as freely as I did in the others. This is fine for any tune with slow moving changes. The Dorian scale is fine, too. Notice how free Jeff gets on his horn with the melody on the out chorus.

G DORIAN SCALE

Art Tatum
Popular from the 1930s to the 1950s, Art Tatum was the most virtuosic and creative pianist of the swing era. His harmonies were a major influence on Herbie Hancock, Chick Corea and many others.

Photo: Institute of Jazz Studies

TOOL 14 : ii-V-I Cycle

The transcription of the piano solo played on the recording of *Make Your Move* can be found on page 45.

This tune is based on a **ii-V-I** cycle, so that you can get familiar with a bit more rapid harmonic movement. As always, practice the left hand first until it is virtually memorized; then learn the right hand, either by reading it or by ear.

To blow in the right hand, the major scale can be used throughout the tune, but it has to be transposed for each "tonic area." (In any **ii-V-I**, the **I** is considered the tonic, so you can also play that blues scale for the entire progression.) Practice this tune, right hand only, as described below:

- D major scale in bars 1–4

- C major scale in bars 5–8

- B♭ major scale in bars 9–12

- D major scale in bars 13–end

Then put hands together and jam!

In the solo, I tried to stick to the major scales of each of the three key areas: D major, C major, B♭ major and back to D major. The more changes you have in a tune, the more you have to deal with each specific change, or at least with each key area.

IMPROVISING TIP:

Now that you're back in the standard tune mode with changes often occurring on every bar, go back and outline the chords like you did in the previous lesson (1-3-5-7-5-3-1, 7-5-3-1-3-5-7, 3-5-7-9-7-5-3, and 9-7-5-3-5-7-9).

The John Coltrane Quartet
Active in the early 1960s, the John Coltrane Quartet was one of the most influential bands in jazz. The pianist, McCoy Tyner, whose early work echoed Bud Powell, later developed new harmonies based on chords voiced in fourths. Tyner wrote several jazz standards such as "Passion Dance" and "You Taught My Heart to Sing."

Photo: Institute of Jazz Studies

TOOL 15 : Minor ii-V-I Cycle

MINOR STEPS Track 16

PLAY 5 TIMES

This tune is also based on a **ii-V-I** harmonic movement, but in the minor. Typically, the minor **ii-V-I** has the following alterations: **ii7(♭5)-V7(♭9)-i7** (the small **i** is used because it's a minor chord).

These voicings can, in the case of the **ii7** and **V7**, be used in major as well; in that case they create more of a rub and give more of a "bebop" flavor.

Learn the left hand until it is fluid, then add the melody. When you can play the tune in tempo, then you can blow on the blues scale that relates to the tonic chord in each four-bar group: C blues scale, bars 1–4; D blues scale, bars 5–8; E blues scale, bars 9–12; and C blues scale, bars 13–16.

Notice the hip voicing of the F7 at the end: F13(♯11) with an added 9. It would be really helpful for you to learn this voicing in every key.

IMPROVISING TIP:

Another interesting scale you could use in the same way as you did the blues scale is the natural minor on each tonic area. For example:

- In bars 1–4 you could play C natural minor.

C Natural Minor

- In bars 5–8 play D natural minor.

D Natural Minor

- In bars 9–12 play E natural minor.

E Natural Minor

- In bars 13–16, play C natural minor.

An A13 chord is also used in bar 12, but this doesn't make bars 9–12 any more challenging to solo on than the previous four-bar phrases. Just treat bars 9–12 as a **ii-V-I** in E minor.

In my solo, I played off the minor scales of each key area: C minor, D minor, E minor and C minor adding some blues-tinged stuff in the first C minor area. Blues is often closer to the minor mode than major, as the flatted third is emphasized.

As always, you should outline each chord using 1-3-5-7 and 3-5-7-9, going up and down. Practice this pattern using ♭5s and ♭9s where indicated in the chord symbols.

TOOL 16 : ii-V Cycle with Bossa Nova Feel

BARRA DA TIJUCA   Track 17

ENTIRE PIECE PLAYED 5 TIMES

FLOWING, MEDIUM BRAZILIAN

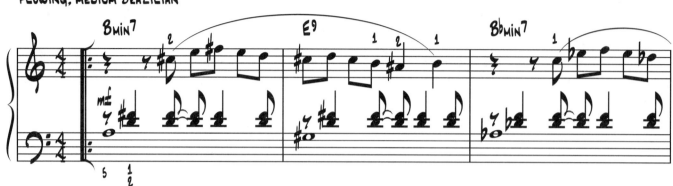

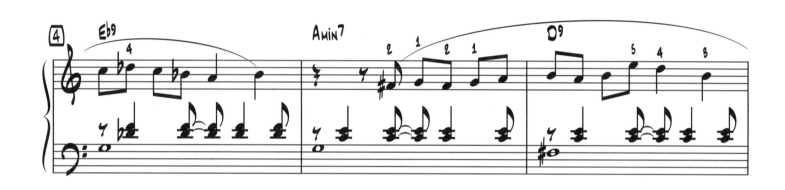

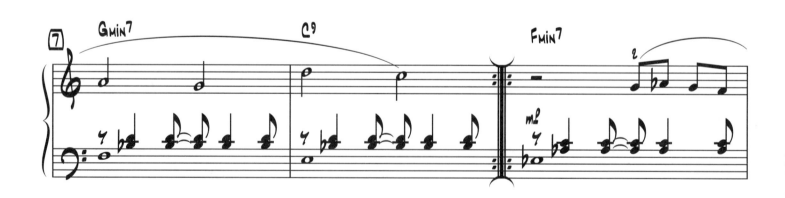

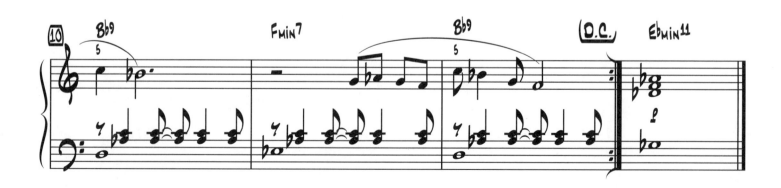

Here is a bossa nova tune with a rather sophisticated harmonic movement. There are several **ii-V** progressions without the resolving **I** (Bmin7 | E9 | B♭min7 | E♭9, etc.). This gives the music a fluidity and a sense of never arriving at a destination. Practice the left hand until it is secure, then add the right hand melody. Then practice 1-3-5-7 and 3-5-7-9 both up and down.

In my solo, I stick pretty much to Mixolydian scales (2 bars each of E, E♭, D and C). Then, I use B♭ Mixolydian on the bridge. I sometimes outline individual changes more specifically for variety.

IMPROVISING TIP:

You can play on the entire **ii-V** using the Mixolydian scale on the **V**. The Mixolydian scale is the same as the major scale but with a minor 7th.

You can also think of it as the scale starting on the fifth degree of the major scale. For example, G Mixolydian is the C major scale starting on G.

- For the progression Bmin7-E9 you can use the E Mixolydian scale or the A major scale.

- For the progression B♭min7-E♭9 you can use the E♭ Mixolydian scale or the A♭ major scale.

Here's an alternate left hand for you to use.

Chick Corea
One of the most innovative pianists in modern jazz, Chick Corea is a brilliant composer and small-group jazz arranger. Like Hancock, he spent much time with electronics in the 1970s and 1980s, but later returned to acoustic jazz and the grand piano.

Photo: Courtesy of Chick Corea Productions

TOOL 17 : Review

PLAY 5 TIMES THROUGH ENTIRE TUNE
MEDIUM UP-SWING

FALL FOLIAGE   Track 18

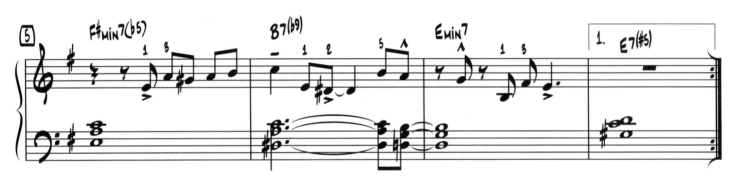

The transcription of the piano solo played on the recording of *Fall Foliage* can be found on page 46.

For your last tune, here's a version of a popular standard with a new melody. Just practice the left-hand voicings along with the track, and then practice the melody by itself. When you are secure, put the hands together. The rhythm section is going to stretch out a bit on this one, so have fun. Now is the time to enjoy yourself, and not worry about making mistakes.

On my solo, I get more into bebop vocabulary (**ii-V** progressions) rather than just outlining scales and arpeggios. Cop a few of these licks and learn them in all keys.

IMPROVISING TIP:

All the tricks you have learned so far will work in this tune.

- Grouping the **ii-V-I** progressions together allows you to play bars 1–4 in G major and bars 5–8 in E harmonic minor.

E Harmonic Minor Scale

- The second half of the tune (bars 10–25) starts out for four bars in E minor (bars 10–13), then four bars in G major (bars 14-17), then the last eight are in E minor (bars 18–25). You could substitute the blues scale for either the harmonic minor or major scales for a different color.

- You can, of course, arpeggiate the chords (1-3-5-7-5-3-1, 7-5-3-1-3-5-7, 3-5-7-9-7-5-3, and 9-7-5-3-5-7-9), or play off the melody, or even just play E blues throughout, and it will sound pretty good.

Bonus Track: Basically Blues
up tempo

This book has really emphasized medium tempo grooves, so I wanted to give you something more burning to play. I don't play a solo, so you have three solo choruses to yourself. Enjoy!

SOMETHING FOR HERBIE

Transcription of the recorded solo improvisation from track 12.

MAKE YOUR MOVE

Transcription of the recorded solo improvisation from track 15.

FALL FOLIAGE

Transcription of the recorded solo improvisation from track 18.

Scale Compendium

The following scales can be used with the chord symbols at the top of each scale group. Next to each scale title is the chromatic alteration (e.g., ♭9, ♯9) contained in each scale.

CMAJ⁷

C MAJOR

C LYDIAN (♯11)

CMIN⁷

C AEOLIAN (NATURAL MINOR) (9, 11)

C HARMONIC MINOR (♮7, 9, 11)

C DORIAN (9, 6/9, 11)

C7 (DOMINANT)

C MIXOLYDIAN (♮9, ♮13)

C LYDIAN/MIXOLYDIAN (♮9, ♯11, ♮13)

C ALTERED (♭9, ♯9, ♯11, ♭13 [or ♯5])

C HALF STEP/WHOLE STEP (♭9, ♯9, ♯11, 13)

C BLUES (works with major, minor and dominant chords)

Discography

Listening to jazz is the most important aspect of learning how to play it. You now know a good deal of the theory, but it's really important to know where the theory came from and how to apply it. This comes from listening to the music.

The great jazz musicians can all sing many of the tunes and solos from their favorite jazz recordings. Though this may seem like a lofty goal, dedicate yourself to learning this music by ear as much as you can.

First, pick out a dozen or so jazz recordings that you really love. Then, select one and spend a week listening to it over and over. Once you start to know the sequence of tunes—when you can predict which tune comes next—practice singing them until you've learned them. If you find this really difficult, pick only a couple of the easiest tunes to start with and just sing along.

Once you can do this easily, play the recording on a boombox next to your piano and try to pick out the notes with just the right hand. Keep doing this until you can play along with the recording without mistakes. Then start to fake the left hand. If the tune is a blues, you can already do this. Make your goal to learn the melody by ear. There is NO shortcut for this.

All of these recordings are available, and nearly all contain 12-bar blues tunes.

Cannonball Adderley: *Quintet in San Francisco*, Fantasy
Kenny Barron: *Green Chimneys*, Criss Cross
Clifford Brown & Max Roach: *On Basin Street*, Emarcy
John Coltrane: *Coltrane's Sound*, Atlantic
John Coltrane: *Giant Steps*, Atlantic
Chick Corea: *Now He Sings, Now He Sobs*, Blue Note
Miles Davis: *Kind of Blue*, Columbia
Miles Davis: *Walkin'*, Original Jazz Classics
Miles Davis: *Workin' and Steamin'*, Fantasy
Bill Evans: *Village Vanguard Sessions*, Fantasy
Tommy Flanagan: *Eclypso*, Enja
Errol Garner: *Concert by the Sea*, Columbia
Benny Goodman: *Carnegie Hall, 1938*, Columbia
Dexter Gordon: *Go*, Blue Note
Herbie Hancock: *Takin' Off*, Blue Note
Barry Harris: *B.H. at the Jazz Workshop*, Riverside
Ahmad Jamal: *But Not For Me*, MCA
Thelonious Monk & John Coltrane, Original Jazz Classics
Lee Morgan: *Sidewinder*, Blue Note
Charlie Parker: *Complete Savoy Sessions*, Savoy
Bud Powell: *Amazing BP*, Blue Note
Sonny Rollins: *Saxophone Colossus*, Fantasy
Sonny Rollins: *Tenor Madness*, Original Jazz Classics
Horace Silver: *Blowin' the Blues Away*, Blue Note
Horace Silver: *Cape Verdean Blues*, Blue Note
McCoy Tyner: *Inception*, Impulse

About the Author

Bill Cunliffe is rapidly becoming one of the best known jazz pianists of today, one who combines lyricism and sensitivity with a fierce sense of swing. He received his master's degree from the Eastman School of Music where he studied with jazz pianist Bill Dobbins, and won several Down Beat Awards for his big band and orchestral pieces.

After three years of teaching at Central State University in Wilberforce, Ohio, he went on the road as pianist and arranger with the Buddy Rich Big Band, doing two tours of Europe with Frank Sinatra. He then played and toured with many of today's greatest jazz musicians including Ray Brown, Joe Henderson, Freddie Hubbard, Art Farmer, James Moody and Joshua Redman. He currently works with his own trio, as well as the Clayton Hamilton Jazz Orchestra, trumpeter Terell Stafford, and flutist Holly Hofmann.

Bill was the 1989 winner of the $10,000 Thelonious Monk International Jazz Piano Award, and has received stipends from the National Endowment for the Arts. His three albums for Warner/Discovery Records all charted in nationwide jazz polls, and his most current albums are *Bill Plays Bud*, a tribute to Bud Powell on Naxos Jazz, and *Satisfaction,* an album of solo jazz piano music on the Azica label. He currently teaches jazz piano at the University of Southern California, and his compositions are available from Kendor Music and the University of Northern Colorado Jazz Press. Bill is a Baldwin Pianos artist, and was Marian McPartland's guest on her famed "Piano Jazz" radio show in June of 1998.

Jeff Clayton is a saxophonist and woodwind player based in Los Angeles. He is co-leader of the Clayton/Hamilton Jazz Orchestra and the Clayton Brothers Quintet, both of whom record for Qwest Records. He has performed and recorded with most of the major figures of modern jazz, as well as pop artists Earth, Wind and Fire and Stevie Wonder.

Mark Ferber is one of the most in-demand drummers on the West Coast and New York and has worked with many of today's best-known jazz artists. He also works with his brother Alan, a virtuoso trombonist who currently resides in the Big Apple. Mark cites Billy Higgins and Bill Stewart as major influences on his playing.

Tom Warrington moved to New York City in the mid-1970s after receiving his master's degree in composition from the University of Illinois. There, he quickly got the call to join the Buddy Rich Big Band, a stint that lasted over two years. After that period, he toured Europe extensively as a performer and clinician.

Tom came to Los Angeles in 1981, and has performed and recorded with a long list of great artists. His playing can be heard on over 100 recordings spanning a wide range of styles, and he continues to play and record with top jazz players.

Writing also plays an increasing role in Tom's activities. In addition to jingle orchestrations and vocal jazz charts, Tom has co-authored *Essential Styles* Books 1 and 2, and the book/CD play-along series *MasterTracks.* He has also written a jazz bass method, *Crawl Before You Walk.*